Sacred Sage Spirit Medicine

Silver Wolf Walks Alone

Published by The WolfWalker Collection
PO Box 2586
Taos, NM 87571

Artwork by Ken Williams

Photography by Billy Stone

Cover and layout design by Kim Wilson

Published 2000
4th edition 2007
ISBN 0-9640229-1-5

I thank my parents,
Hildegarde and Russell,
for being that
which they are.

Our Mother the Earth

Our Mother, who is the Earth,
honored are you by us.
Your kingdom is here
your Way to be followed by us.

Send us each day
the blessings you bestow
and forgive us for any harm
we may have caused
as we atone for that harm.

Lead us not into judgment
but deliver us to balance once again.
For your Way is the Glory of us
the Love of us,
and the Grace of us.

Contents

PREFACE

**God is absolute Truth
I am relative truth
My commitment is to Truth,
not to being consistent.**

Gandhi

In 1992, I wrote Sacred Sage How It Heals, a small booklet that told about the healing attributes of the sage plant, artemisia tridentata. Sage, in its different forms, has been used by indigenous peoples and herbalists for hundreds of years as an internal purifier in the form of teas, and as a ceremonial purifier in the form of smoke. I wrote Sacred Sage How it Heals during a time of great upheaval in my life. The beginning of this upheaval seemed to coincide with early but natural menopause.

I remember that day in the gynecologists office when he read the test results to me like the headlines of a boring news article. Without even looking up for my response, he began to write out a prescription for HRT (hormone replacement therapy). He also slid across his shiny desk a pamphlet about HRT. After reading a few of the "side effects" namely; cancer, blood clots, etc. I asked what would happen if I did not take the hormones. From his thin lips came a textbook answer, "early bone loss, sweats, mood swings, leg cramps, loss of sexual appetite, dryness in the vaginal area, and maybe uterine cancer due to a building up of the lining," I got a second opinion, but not an answer more to my liking. So I chose the latter list of "things to look forward to".

My irrational and unusual behavior, along with a personality change, was given many labels - a hormone imbalance, a mid-life crisis, a depression, a nervous breakdown, a stressful life style, an unhappy marriage (I was quite happy with it), and last but not least, a psychic said I had become a walk-in.

My life seemed to speed up uncontrollably, and I found my self questioning everything and every one in my life. In a matter of a few short months I was like a different person. I wanted answers to all the deep questions of our lives. My cohorts only wanted to know who was playing in Wimbledon, and which island they were going to for the next vacation. I wanted to right all the wrongs of the world, clean up the environment, meet the aliens, heal the sick, and find the one true religion because Christianity had let me down. And I wanted it NOW. I was even willing to give up everything I had at thirty two years of age and begin my quest for knowledge. My marriage ended, old friends vanished, family members looked at me queerly. I closed down my business and my only means of income. I took up spiritual pursuits, attended metaphysical classes, and devoured all the books I could read. I wanted the answers to why I was here! In retrospect, I was having a spiritual emergency. By the grace of God, I did not listen to anyone and try to "get some professional help". I did not consciously know why this was happening or how to go about answering this call. I believe that early menopause was part of the grand plan for my life and a jump start to my rather early quest for self-realization. The eternal was emerging to cleanse the false, illusory personality.

From 1987 to 1996 I continued to travel from Richmond, Virginia to the Southwest. Many incredible people were placed in my path. Some brought "blessens" and some brought "lessons". Each trip brought me closer to a reality. Someday I would move to Taos, New Mexico, home of my beloved sage. I did just that in April of 1996.

With many silver hairs, lessons learned, and badges earned, I saw that life was about a stream of events that allowed us to make choices. These choices either moved us closer to conscious soul growth or created more unconscious patterns which WOULD BE dealt with later.

The journey shared in this book is from personal experience. It is my wish to share with the reader how sage (artemisia) has once again been my ally in spiritual growth. Is it possible for a simple plant such as sage, to have such an effect on a person's life? Our medicines are usually derivatives of plants, used to cure all sorts of physical ailments. But, can the Spirit of a plant have an effect on the Spirit of a human?

Rumi, a thirteenth century Muslim mystic said, "lovers of God, sometimes a door opens, and a human being becomes a way for grace to come through...". Indeed, many humans have been messengers of God's grace. Also true, is that any of God's creations can be doors that open to his Grace. It is no coincidence that the common name of sage was given to the plant artemisia tridentata. Sage means "marked by great wisdom and calm judgment". I now live among the great old sagebrush and continue to harvest sage. I use it for many purposes. The spirit of these old ones are continuously teaching me.

SACRED SAGE Spirit Medicine is a continuation of the first book. SACRED SAGE How it Heals. Spirit Medicine is about my personal journey "home" and the teachings received through the constant companion of the spirit of artemisia. Throughout the book I will use both names of this plant. Sage, being its common name, and artemisia, being its true Latin name. This book can be read without reading the first volume, but some readers may find it helpful to know more about the physical healing attributes of this plant and its ceremonial uses.

You will see that what is talked about and what is felt is nothing more than universal truth. No magic, no frills, no gimmicks, no shortcuts to enlightenment. It already resides at "home" inside you. Have you been still long enough to recognize it? Have you stayed at "home" long enough to let the mud settle and allow the answer to birth itself? My hope in sharing these personal reflections is that they will also become doors to God's Grace for those whose path crosses sacred sage.

For those of you who feel a special relationship with a plant, I encourage you to pursue its spiritual message through a plan of your own or through some of the suggestions I offer here.

Part One

Taos... Home to Sacred Sage

**For things to reveal themselves to us,
we need to be ready to abandon our
views about them.**

Thich Nhat Hanh

Taos, New Mexico is home to sacred sage. Resting at an elevation of seven thousand feet, with temperatures ranging from below 0 degrees to above 100, it provides the right conditions. Sage can be found growing south of Taos and running all the way up the San Luis valley into Colorado. Artemisia found her way here, by traveling in the wool of the sheep grazing the plains of the San Luis Valley. The valley's grasslands were decimated due to overgrazing. She (I will refer to artemisia in the feminine form) is the main vegetation on the valley mesa, holding what precious topsoil is left to the earth. She provides food and shelter to the animals and birds of the mesa desert. Most of the sacred sage that is used around the U.S. comes from here. To understand the warrior spirit of this sage (artemisia tridentata) it is important to know something about its home. She is a direct reflection of her home and the peoples of Taos.

Taos, some people say, means red willow in Tewa, the language of the Taos Pueblo people. They continue to speak their unwritten language as well as English and Spanish, and seek balance between the modern influences and traditional life. This has been their home for over one thousand years, with the existing pueblo (town) being built around 1350. Their predecessors, the Anasazi Indians, were in the valley prior to this period, but little is known about them. They are, by nature, a quiet agrarian people, but life has sent them to battle for their homelands and culture with both the Spanish Conquistadors and the Anglo invasions.

Taos has been a mecca for a wide variety of people, all coming here throughout history for its beauty and trade. Taos has been a crossroads for the southwest for hundreds of years. Indian trails led here from all directions, Spanish explorers came in 1540 and the French and American fur trappers came in the 1700's. It is a melting pot of three cultures that have, somehow, managed to survive side by side even with continued clashes. Now, in present day, it is even more of a spiritual melting put with all the major religions represented here and Buddhism is finding Taos a welcoming home. A famous quote of old Doc Martin, the famous physician from the early 1900's, tells it all about the mystic of Taos. In a conversation with a New York reporter, about a murder that took place here, The newsman inquired, "Who's the police commissioner up there?"

"There ain't none." replied the doctor.
"Then, who's the police chief?"
"We haven't got one."
"Well who's in charge up there?"
"God's in charge up here." answered Martin, "God's in charge of everything that happens in Taos."[*1]

Taos is a high desert, mountainous area of about 10,000 people. It is not likely that you will get here by mistake. There is no easy or fast way into Taos. No matter what direction you come, it is a challenging drive. The Sangre de Christos mountains, desert mesas, Rio Grande Gorge or river must be crossed and at a careful pace. The most famous route from Santa Fe brings you up the

*1 - pg 25, "A Brief History of Taos", by F.R. Romero & Neil Poese 1992. Kit Carson Historical Museums.

Santa Fe highway that follows along the Rio Grande river. The road is narrow, winding, and sometimes very treacherous during inclement weather. With steep mountains on one side and the river on the other it is difficult to keep your eyes on the road. Each bend in the road offers another visual delight to even the unartistic eye! At the top of this ascent is one of the most photographed panoramic views in the Southwest, Upon my first experience, I stopped the car and wept, I thought that I had found Shangri La!

From this point on the highway, you see the immense crack in the earth (the Gorge and river) that stretches to the North. Miles of sage covered mesa span either side of the Gorge and the incredible Sangre de Christos mountains stand as sentinels to the East. All this is displayed in a continuously challenging and unworldly light show, In the summer, expect to see double rainbows daily. Sunsets that are painted but, never captured, by every artist that visits. In the winter, clouds can hover and caress the mountains for days sometimes, lifting up to expose their precious occupant, like a mother who adoringly checks on here sleeping baby. Other times, during a harsh Arctic blast, the clouds seem to block entrance to the Taos Mountains ensuring them of a much needed rest.

Coming from Angel Fire, the Taos Canyon road is 26 miles of narrow winding turns down the mountains and through Carson National Forest.

If you take the back route, No. 285, from Española through Carson, you hit a narrow dirt road. It feels like a washboard and tumbles and nose dives into the Rio Grande Gorge. It is not a route for the faint-hearted.

The 64 east route from Tres Piedras brings you across the desert mesa and across the Rio Grande Gorge bridge, which is 700 feet above the Rio Grande river. This small two lane bridge is invisible until you are practically on it. The only words to describe this experience is "Oh my God!!"

One of my attractions to Taos was the rich diversity of ethnic peoples. Growing up in a predominantly middle white class neighborhood, fueled my later desires to travel the roads less taken. I have lived overseas in third world nations and on the Navajo reservation at times. Living in Taos, NM is like living out of the US but still under its protective umbrella. No one lives here unless you have some sort of adventuresome spirit. It is like a third world nation going through harsh growing pains. The last 10 years seem to have brought both the good and the challenging aspects of civilization to Taos.

Most people come here as tourists for the natural beauty and the outdoor adventures, art galleries, and historical places. Some people come to do business with the artists.

If you find yourself coming here to live, I believe you are on the precipice of major change. And I mean this in more ways than one!! Most people who live here will tell you that it has a mystical quality that just can't be explained. When sitting in a local coffee shop or on the Plaza, it is not a surprise to hear another story about how someone came to Taos and never left. Many people come here because of an inner guidance - just an act of faith. This is not a town that people come to for a job transfer or career opportunity. It is difficult for most people to make a satisfactory living in Taos. There are many strong, talented warrior men and women in Taos, who are very committed to personal growth and higher consciousness. What this place lacks in financial security is far outweighed by its natural beauty and spiritual circles. It is a place of transformation. How that transformation takes place may not be as you would like it. Many people here think of Taos mountain as a living entity that spits you out or swallows you up The sagebrush also does its work. The Dark Night of the Soul just might have an appointment with you here in Taos.

Having lived here four years now, I would not tell anyone to move here. It is a place that will call YOU! It is a place for serious healing and conscious growth. Taos can strip you naked and show you all of your baggage! It will show you baggage that you did not even know you had! It will put other peoples baggage in front of you and you will pick it up!! You will try to throw it out the car window during a trip to the lonely desert mesa, but don't you know, it will be back in your yard the next morning, compliments of the wily coyotes!!!

Taos is a place that can stretch you if you come to live here. Some people come looking for an easy spiritual adventure and leave disillusioned. Be ready to accept the unseen and unexpected. Be ready for the ultimate test, the taming of the ego. Who and what you did elsewhere is not necessarily what you will be here. I have met many people who have come here because they were guided by an unknown force. They left behind them a life that was no longer satisfying. When the ego takes that final blow, you are ripe for transformation. Ready to shed the parts of yourself which no longer are appropriate for true destiny. This is the biggest adventure of life. This is the opportunity to meet self. Who am I? Is it coincidence that the word Tao, in Chinese, means the way or path? It is the law that governs all of existence and nonexistence. It is the way of balance, accepting what is good or bad, and finding a way to live with it harmoniously. The Tao is also a way to get lost or the way to not know. Sometimes we need to get lost, in order to get rid of thinking that we DO know what to do, especially if it is self-serving.

Perhaps, Taos is a place where a magical alchemy of energies come together in order to create a place for personal freedom. It is a spiritual power place that has representation from all the major religious groups. If you are open to a higher guidance taking over, it will. You will advance, but maybe not in ways that you thought. I could never have written my life as it has unfolded over the last four years. If you are so attached to a view that nothing else could be possible, you have not allowed for a basic truth .... CHANGE!!!!

Taos is old and wise
and tough and resilient.
Over more than four centuries, it has felt
wave after dynamic wave of influence,
and has absorbed them all
into its always outgoing vitality.

Claire Morrill "A Taos Mosaic"

The Unfolding of a New Age

**Making each present day,
a conscious effort to care
for the planet, others, and yourself,
is leaving no past that is regretted,
and a future that can be lived.**

Silver Wolf Walks Alone

     The unfolding of a new age has been upon us now for many years. We have been feeling the birth contractions of the Aquarian Age and experiencing the death moans of the Piscean Age. This cusp period is due to the merging of one age into another. As in all aspects of nature there is no distinct line of demarcation but instead, a blending of the seasons. Because of the Precision of the Equinoxes, the world is influenced by a different sign of the Zodiac every 2000 years. This creates an even greater cycle called The Great Year which is about 26,000 years long. Here, each of the twelve zodiac signs, has an influence over human destiny and we see great civilizations rise and fall. During the Great Year, we have wise ones, the "Illuminate" watch over human progress, sometimes taking an active role in guiding the material plane. Sometimes the wise ones withdraw to the inner planes so that we may learn through direct experience how to manifest spiritual harmony on the physical plane. During periods of time when the wise ones control the positions of power, they predict the new age and prepare the minds of the people for this influence. These periods of transition were much smoother than our present transition which has been accomplished with many injustices and bloodshed.

The Piscean Age taught us many lessons. On the positive note, it ushered in spiritual wisdom, inspiration, compassion and universal love. On the downbeat, we experienced chaos, confusion, delusion, fear, escapism and separation. Jupiter's influence, that of higher mind and consciousness, manifested itself in the church and institutions. However, because of our present state of human development we responded to Jupiter's gifts with a lower consciousness that created abuse in these institutions. For example, generations upon generations have given away their personal power to these institutions. The Church became a major influence to western civilization. Its theme became guilt, sacrifice, and persecution. We were to blindly follow the dictates of the ecclesiastical councils as if they were the Divine Word. Taking responsibility for the care of our own spirit was given away. Faith alone was to be followed and scientific explanations scoffed at. Then, we gave our personal power over to governments. They gladly took it saying that they, an elite few, indeed knew how to run our everyday lives better than we do. Then, we gave our physical bodies over to medical science. Instead of practicing a healthy life-style we got lazy and said, "I'll just buy medical insurance and if something happens the doctors can fix it."

This continuous lack of personal responsibility (escapism) created abusive institutions. And now people have been blaming everything outside of ourselves for the woes of society. Victimhood was created. And with victimhood comes an even greater sense of denial, and loss of personal power. By personal power, I mean self respect.

We have been dealing with generations of fear. It has been taught by the church, government, medical institutions, business, and even the family. Secrets have abounded and truth has taken a back seat. It was a way to control and harness the human spirit and use it for the benefit of a few.

Neptune, also influenced the Piscean Age with its task to dissolve unconscious patterns from former lives. This was necessary in order to move on to new experiences. Chaos and confusion was experienced, because of resistance to the unconscious becoming conscious. Neptune worked internally so that we were forced to look within for the Truths.

The Aquarian Age has already given us a taste for the future with the incredible advances in technology. The computers, internet, world wide web, satellites, is just the beginning. We will move into the realm of mind with thought transference, and thought projection. Perhaps, also the ability to communicate with nature and the other realms.

The symbol of Aquarius is the water bearer. It represents the pouring out of knowledge from the super conscious to all of humanity. Water represents intuition. All knowledge already exists here. We have to uncover it. The next 2000 years will assist man in unfolding his mental vehicles and bring about the full development of humanity's mental stature. All this sounds exciting, but will we stay conscious to the fact that any of these gifts can be abused? Will the computer replace person to person contact, making the Aquarian vision of world brotherhood, one of the mind rather than the heart? Hopefully, there are enough teachers present to remind us that the cool, dispassionate, reasoning mind must be tempered with the warmth of a loving heart. From this marriage, intuition awakens and the ability to sense the Truth appears, no longer hidden by the arrogance of the ego.

The Buddha recognized that the three harmful attitudes of ignorance, attachment, and anger create the actions we engage in; such as killing, stealing, lying, greed and envy. These actions will not end until the attitude ends. Has enough of the unconscious patterns in our lives been exposed so that we can come forward and take RESPONSIBILITY for our lives? Can we acknowledge as a human race, that together we created the very actions that caused our own suffering and the suffering of others? This recognition is what frees us from victimhood and now allows us to see that we always have choice.

The Aquarian Age is a 2000 year period of growth that is dedicated to openly communicating the Truth; to studying the unconscious so as to make it conscious; to sharing our fears in order to understand their illusory themes; and to seeing the pearl of truth that strings all religions together, rather than viewing them as dangerously different. It is an enormous time of personal and universal transformation. It is not just for this planet but intergalactic. It is a cleansing that must be experienced for the individual soul as well as the betterment of all mankind.

America has very special evolutionary and karmic obligations. We are the largest melting pot of cultures and relations in the world. This magical alchemy took place for a very special reason. We have had a great opportunity to live next door to an Afro-American, Mexican, Vietnamese, Irish, German, Italian, Russian, Iranian or anyone else to learn and experience the beauty of their way. Only in America have we had the opportunity of going to a Catholic church or a Jewish synagogue, a Hindu temple or Buddhist stuppa or a native sweat lodge. We have had hundreds of years to learn, better than anyone, this business of individual expression and to develop the ability to accept each others differences. Although we have not always done well with it, each generation can do better. This Aquarian age can finally bind us all as relations. Only through this rise in conscious behavior will the Christian sit with the Muslim, who will sit with the Jew, who will sit with the Hindu who will sit with the Buddhist who will sit with the atheist. All will recognize each other as different strips of the same rainbow. Finally, we Americans can usher into this planet a compassionate understanding of differences within the ties that bind us.

For those who are conscious and can read between the lines, it is obvious that much of what has been created over the last 1000 years is no longer serving us in a healthy way. This planet cannot live with the physical and mental pollution we are giving it.

For those who have had to face many challenges in their lives, they can now be assured that they have experienced those challenges to gain the strength that is needed to continue. Living in the past and ruminating over actions already done will be dangerous. Always hoping for the future to hurry and come, will be disappointing. What is needed is a balance. The balance is living in the present. The present is made from past moments already lived and future moments being dreamed. They are actually all the same and occurring simultaneously. We can live in the present successfully, by recognizing the past behaviors that have held us back and clearing them. The future will come of its own accord, because it always has. You can save for it, and prepare for it, and worry about it, but that is no insurance for challenge-free futures. Making each present day a conscious effort to care for the planet, others, and yourself is leaving no past that is regretted and a future that can be lived.

**The Master sees things as they are,
without trying to control them.
She lets them go their own way
and resides at the center of the circle.**

Lau Tzu

Many metaphysicians, and indigenous peoples, talk of the Four Corners area, as a very powerful vortex of energy. It will be a light center for future years to come during and after the great changes of our times. It is a place of harmony, peace, and self-transformation.

One of the largest stands of artemisia lives near here, stretching from south of Taos, running up the San Luis mesa valley to southern Colorado. Artemisia has a warrior spirit that brings purification and transformation to those who seek it. She is the herb of the Aquarius Age. She purifies body and mind so that old patterns dissolve and new experiences arise. She is master at exposing the illusions of the ego and is the huntress for the Truth.

Part Two

The Commitment

The moment one definitely commits oneself,
then Providence moves too.
All sorts of things occur
to help one
that would never otherwise have occurred.

A whole stream of events issues from that decision.
Raising in one's favor
all manner of unforeseen incidents
and meetings and material assistance
which no man could have dreamed
would have come his way.....

A few years after using artemisia in ceremony and physical healing, I had a desire to go deeper into her healing abilities. When the decision had been made to move to Taos, I knew that I had to live within the sage so that I could build a relationship with her. She was very much alive for me. After harvesting, the aroma of her oil on my hands would open the lines of communication. I felt that the spirit of this incredible plant had wisdom to share.

I got in touch with my teacher and asked for his help in learning how to talk with this plant. His response was as usual, a question, "Do you see and hear first with your physical eyes and ears or do you use another set?" Not being able to match wits with him, I did not know how to answer. I closed my eyes and thought very hard. Then I said, "I see and hear first with my physical senses." He very quickly said, "Then why did you close your eyes and use your mind's eye to see or hear the answer to the question? To learn about the spirit of a plant you will use different eyes and ears. Intuitive eyes and ears... a sense that we all have, but few have taken the time to develop.

I can not teach you what you are asking for. But I can be a guide. You have not met the spirit of sage because you were not ready to accept her gift. She has been a guide for you these last four years. She will come and this time you will not escape her!!

He told me that to really learn about the spiritual messages of a plant ally I would have to woo that plant as I would a lover. I would have to trust the messages I received as if it was coming from a best friend. I would have to care for this ally as if it were my child. I would have to use this plant in many ways in my daily life. I would call upon this plant in time of need as well as celebrate it during times of abundance. In other words, this plant ally would become as important to me as my relationship with my Creator. I would ingest this plant, smoke this plant, wash with this plant, tend this plant, sweat with this plant, vision quest with this plant, carry it with me, sleep with it near by, dream it, draw it, sit with it, and anything else I could do to create as complete a relationship with this plant as I could.

Before this began, however, I needed to know how to recognize the "inner eyes and ears".

The Realization

Who is the Holy Spirit?
The Holy Spirit is a compassionate
outpouring of the Creator and the son.
This is why when we on earth pour out our
compassion and mercy from the depths of our
hearts and give to the poor and the broken,
to that extent do we resemble the Holy Spirit.

Mechtild of Magdeburg

It had been months since my move to Taos. Mundane life had taken over and I was distressed about my lack of time spent with my true purpose for coming here. I decided to go for a walk amongst the sage and along the edge of the Rio Grande gorge.

I was gathering sage and thinking about my commitment to building a relationship with her. Finding this inner voice my teacher had talked about was not easy. I was feeling doubt and confusion. He was also not one to tell you how to do things. He would say, "If you want something bad enough, you will go after it. How you do it differs with everyone. Two people can want the same thing, but go after it in two entirely different ways. And what happens along the way is often more important than the success or failure of the mission."

How does one trust this inner voice completely? I heard my teachers voice again, "remember the sweat lodge teachings." When you are in a state of imbalance, go back to the basics. The four foundation footsteps.... Love, Charity, Faith & Hope. These footsteps are the basics to each and every endeavor. They will show you that gratitude is a must for each "lesson or Bless'on" in your life. These are here for a deeper reason, that may not be apparent yet.

I had walked for quite a while and my thoughts were inter-rupted by the cool, moist air of an early morning melt. I shivered and zipped my jacket, as El Niño had passed by us the night before, dropping a much needed blanket of snow on the mesa. I faced the East where the sun had silently risen above the Sangre de Cristo mountains. I looked down into the giant gorge and heard the sound of the rushing Rio Grande river. I had been following an ancient lava flow to this point, whose rocks had been rounded and worn by the desert's winds and flash floods. At the end, where it poured forth into the gorge, it formed a perfect chair that beckoned me to sit down. I started to relax and let go of my mental battle with the "inner voice" issue. The magic of the land took over.

I closed my eyes and started a meditation. After a few minutes I felt a stirring in my root chakra and suddenly was pulled down deep into the bed rock. I quickly left my physical body and became liquid, molten lava that burst forth, back up and out of the ancient lava chair. My new container did not feel foreign, but instead I felt relief and a sense of freedom. Accepting this dramatic change in my physical form, I quickly lost control and started to flow off the rocky chair. My fiery liquid mass flowed red hot and gravity was now the master of my fate. Downward and outward I poured, until I took flight over the side of the gorge, as a river of blazing molten rock.

In that instant, I felt like pure consciousness and was taken to a place called the "Hall of Records". Before me came, at great speed, snapshots of faces... children, men and women. Each one brought a wave of knowingness that I had experienced all those bodies. I was man and woman. I was black and brown, and white and red. I had been rich and poor, very old and very young. With each face I had a knowing about a wrong that I had committed or a wrong that had been done to me. Everything that had happened in all those incarnations was necessary. There was no judgment from a higher source, but instead, the judgement came from me. My spirit was judge and jury. Much of the suffering endured had been unknowingly self-inflicted. The guides around me offered love and support, but said they could never interrupt the free will granted me. I saw even my intentions as deeds, and realized the importance of impeccability in thought and word.

When I returned to my physical body there was a greater understanding of who "I" really was... The ego "I" was very temporary and changed with every new body that I took on. It was all the illusions of the physical, emotional and mental bodies. The ego was the voice that judged all accomplishments and failures and would do anything to stay in control. It wants to be the master of this material world and our true identity is masked by this temporary and ever changing ego. Ego is doubt, fear, and confusion.

The journey to the Hall of Records showed me that our TRUE ESSENCE is still consciousness that sees and breathes through all creations. This consciousness is not relative, but absolute. It is the force that flows through all. The divine is within us and every other creation making everything sacred and mysterious. We are to know the glory of God in our very being and all of life.

I knew that I was to never lose the awe that life provides on a daily basis. Awe provides the spice of life, like cinnamon and nutmeg flavor an apple pie. We are here to learn the Truth about self through ourselves and everything around us. I saw that Truth could be found in something as simple as a sprig of sage.

The experience at the gorge led me to the knowing that I had been afraid of really knowing artemisia. I was too afraid to know the real me. I would have to let go of the me I thought I was. I now felt ready. Once I had admitted this to myself I was free to explore her deeply. I arranged for a vision quest with my teacher in August.

(Note: to those who do not know what a sweat lodge or vision quest is, this is a very brief explanation.

Many tribal peoples will send an individual out into nature alone, with no food or water, in order to receive a vision or answer to one's question. The quest can be done anywhere that is quiet and secure. Sometimes on top of a mountain, or inside a vision pit in the ground, or in a sweat lodge. A medicine person should prepare the questor ahead of time and will often stay out of sight, but nearby to the questor to provide protection.

A sweat lodge is a structure made from tree saplings, stuck in the ground in a circle and bent over into the middle of the circle and tied together. It looks like an upside down basket. The lodge is then covered with blankets so that it is dark inside. Hot rocks from a fire pit outside are brought into the lodge. Water is poured onto the rocks and steam is produced, making its inhabitants sweat. Herbs are also put in the lodge. Prayers and songs are offered up to the Divine. The people are purified internally and externally - born anew once again!

The Quest

Hunt the inner wilderness.

Silver Wolf Walks Alone

.

My teacher told me many times - to know that you don't know is good, to surrender to it, to be quiet, still, and unmoving in the face of not knowing will bring self realization. How many times I would hear this and not know what he was talking about. He told me that I had not been able to match her (sage). I now was full of anticipation and eagerness to quest.

It was August and I had been at my Navajo family's dwelling for a week. I was preparing for the quest in the Chuska mountains with a cleansing fast and helping with the items needed for the quest. I was going to quest inside the sweat lodge for as long as it took to receive vision.

My teacher had been acting most unusual the whole time I had been there. Either ignoring me or irritating me. This quest was important to me and I wanted everything to be done honorably. Instead, he was being the buffoon and acting like nothing was sa-

20

cred. Finally, the day had come to start the quest. I was more than anxious, and frustrated with the constant delays and the buffoonery. He had told me that morning, we would be leaving shortly, so get ready. Six hours later, all six kids and my teacher and his wife and dogs are in the old truck. One tire was missing lug nuts so my teacher wired it on to the axle, said a prayer and threw in some cedar. The kids loaded in food and some toys and I assumed that they and the goodies would be dropped off somewhere along the way. The atmosphere was once again trivial and seemingly uncaring that I was preparing for this most important quest.

We finally entered the mountains and everyone was still with us. I was about to pop with frustration and decided to just write this experience off to my own foolishness. I should have packed up and left after a few days into the visit. Perhaps, I had come at a bad time or I had misjudged this teacher all together. My mind came up with all kinds of scenarios, but I decided to see this through, no matter what.

We got the lodge built just before nightfall and it was filled with the most potent smelling sage I had ever harvested. The Chuska mountains had big stands of healthy sage due to good rainfall. My teacher told me to go and get ready and then meet him in front of the lodge. When I got there, he was playing with the kids and his wife was putting out a big spread of food. Once again, this unnecessary delay was not my version of this serious event. I was utterly disappointed with everyone and burning red with rage. This had gone from buffoonery to madness. What was he doing? I was so angry that I couldn't speak, and I couldn't think. I crawled into the lodge and started to cry. It was all ruined and by my own teacher. It was over... this supposed relationship. I would be better off alone. All of a sudden, the flap opened and he crawled in. I sat in silence waiting for some kind of instruction or explanation for everything that had transpired over the last 12 days. Instead, he started singing and picking at his toenails. I couldn't take anymore. This was a disgrace! I yelled at him and asked him to get out of the lodge and take his family with him. I deserved better than this. I had been a good student and why was he doing this to me!!

He became very silent and still. His whole demeanor changed before me. He started a prayer in Diné that I recognized. When he finished, he looked at me and said, "OK, now you are on your own, as you want." He crawled back out of the lodge and loaded me up with hot rocks and a bucket of water. If I needed more, I was to come to the fire and get more, but not go outside the circle. He raised the flap one more time and said, "Take my eagle fan, you will need it. I should take all my medicine out of here because of your attitude toward this quest."

"What!!!! MY attitude!" I said.

Within five minutes, there was not a sound or movement outside the lodge. In fact, it became somewhat eerie. I was so upset my stomach hurt and my pulse was pounding. My mind was racing through the whole week trying to make some sense of it. I tried to pray and I could not even do that because of my uncontrollable anger at this predicament. Here I sat. Nothing, not one iota of this made amy sense! I started to cry and this didn't produce any relief. What did I do wrong here? I did everything as I was to do. I went over and over and over every detail until I wanted to cut my head off and throw it in with the rocks.

I laid down on the bed of sage and tore a piece off. I had to get some control over myself so that I could relax into this quest. I started hewing the sage and tried singing a song. I was sweating profusely and I hadn't even put water on the rocks yet. It was hot, but nothing like I was used to. I tried to concentrate on the littlest things to get some sense of balance so I could move forward in this quest. Nothing... nothing... nothing... then nausea. The most severe nausea I had ever experienced in my life. I doubled over with pain and started heaving. My mind said, "no wonder, with everything you have gone through, you should be upset."

I didn't know what to do. I was now feeling very disoriented and physically weak on top of the emotional upheaval. I laid on the sage but its pungency was overwhelming and I thought that I should throw it all out. It had never been offensive to me before, but this time I couldn't take its strong penetrating odor. Once again I blamed my teacher for putting too much sage in the lodge. It was making me sicker and sicker and again I heaved. There was nothing left in my body because of the fast, and now the dry heaves had taken hold. My body was uncontrollably shaking. I reached around the lodge floor looking for the water bucket. I grabbed the ladle and felt the cool water... a little drink and maybe I would feel better. I sipped the water and suddenly was repulsed again. It was infused with sage!! Another wave of nausea came and took hold. I got on my knees, blindly trying to scurry over to the door. I knocked the bucket over on the rocks. The whole lodge quickly filled with steam and the sage came alive. The essence of the artemisia had been freed, and now in her full glory, her ultimate assault upon my ego could begin. I was totally overwhelmed by the sage essence. Fear arose and I started to feel a warrior presence. I felt like I was going to die... something must be wrong... I had to get out of there!

I reached for the door but it wasn't there. I didn't remember moving that far away so I started to crawl, reaching and groping for the door. Oh, how I wanted to get out and now!!! I felt like the lodge was filling up with something besides me, something much bigger and stronger than me. I was in no shape to meet it. Where was the door? No door! I crawled further reaching into the darkness, feeling the saplings and the blankets, but no door. Everything was tied down good. I tried to pull the blankets up along the bottom, but there was something heavy holding the canvas down. I felt one more excruciating heave and I collapsed on the sage. "No more", I remember saying, "please, no more!"

I can't tell you what happened after that. Did I pass out from exhaustion and illness? Did I fall asleep? Did I enter another realm? I don't know. I remember stillness, silence, and the inability to physically move. I remember a feeling of detachment to whatever was going to happen. I had surrendered completely to my body, my mind, my emotions. I thought I was laying down, but found out later I was sitting up with the eagle fan in my hand.

Slowly, the vision unfolded. I had a sense that I was in the underworld. A youthful figure came walking towards me. I could not get a sense of gender because it seemed to be changing; sometimes male and sometimes female... androgynous, delicate, but strong. The face was beautiful and young but old with wisdom. He/She carried a bow and arrow that flashed with light when it moved. She/He was flanked by an array of forest animals. I had this sense that this young being was coming AT, not TO me. I could not move. Fear rose and then fell. I watched this person coming closer and closer. I was sometimes blinded by the shiny bow and arrow, but I could see that he/she was lifting it to his head and looking down the shaft of the arrow at me. Everything stopped. No thought , no feeling, no movement....... and then a sense of peace.

The peace was one of total surrender to the present and to the knowing that I was ready to die. I sat and stared and he/she stood and stared. I don't know how long in time we stayed like this.

There was no time. Then I realized that the arrow had left its home and was headed for its mark. In slow motion, I watched this shinny arrow come closer and closer. The archer had not moved nor had I. Now the arrow was coming and suddenly it was right before me suspended in the air. I remember examining it with detached interest. It was silver and much smaller than I thought. It was made with precision and had no seams or marks of any kind. Was this work of art to be the weapon of my death? With enormous difficulty and weightedness, I tried to lift my arm and touch this thing of beauty but in a flash it pierced straight through my chest. I gasped and grabbed the point of entry only to realize that there was no pain, no blood, no wound. There was an ecstatic moment. I looked up for the archer, my assassin, but there was no one there. The knowing inside me was one of immense gratitude for my "beloved assassin!" I was free.

The androgynous being appeared next to me and took my hand. For the next 24 hours I was taken through realms not of this world. My guide walked with me through the inner wilderness of mind showing me the paradox of who I thought I was. I learned to embrace all parts of myself including that which is capable of destruction. I had to BE IT completely in order to no longer give it power over me. To understand it, so I could free it. This was the wilderness... the inner wilderness, the only wilderness that exists.

This was my guide to the inner self, the Original Self, She/He impressed upon me that life is about finding this original self by pealing away the layers of illusion that had been brought on by cultural, familial, or sexist demands. For me, artemisia had become the door to freedom.

My guide was like the wolf who was strong, confident, playful and ready to chase or be chased. She/He was faithful to self, curious, protective, territorial and nurturing.

We began the hunt and my guide lead me to the underworld. It was in brilliant red. One door after another was opened to reveal its contents. The first door opened. The people were part human and part animal. One woman whose energy alone told me she was a master, beckoned me to enter. I held the eagle fan in front of me hoping that this was just illusion. Her power was overwhelming and her gaze alone made me look down. I could not meet her eyes. My guide, however, said that doors were initiations. And in order to continue through the underworld this goddess must first be approached. "Trust her as you have trusted me." This goddess had the ability to communicate directly to my soul. She knew me. Her message was, "Know your dark side." I understood that she was telling me to embrace it so that it no longer controlled me. Do not fear this side of human nature. It exists. Fearing it will only give it power. Face it head on and destroy the fear.

I entered a hallway that was again red and everything about it was over toned in red. Many doors were there and I started to open each one. With my eagle fan in front of me, I faced the unknown terrain of the deepest inner self.

There was the door of lust. A man who I was attracted to luring me into an affair that I knew would serve nothing but sexual pleasure. The door of self-pity opened to see a woman as a rather pathetic person, ruminating over all the hurts she had acquired. Her story went on and on about broken promises, appreciation never received, abusive lovers, long hard hours of work. Another door opened, that of temptation. It held nothing but a table. On this table was a bag of gold coins. I looked around this room and saw no one. How easy it would be to take this bag of gold coins. I would be rich. All my problems would be solved! With each door my guide would simply look at me but telepathically send me a message that said, "If you want this, pick it up. If you don't want it, leave it alone." Most of what I saw was about the humans lower self, and the suffering our decisions have caused. I would raise the eagle fan and cover my face from the scenes that I did not want. Many doors followed. To each one I raised the eagle fan no longer wanting to be part of the drama. This journey had made it very clear to me that I and only I was responsible for the choices in my life.

At the last door my guide and I sat down. She talked to me about her/his androgynous nature. She said that in her femaleness she was the protector of women and was willing to slay anyone who would threaten to defile, demean, or destroy femaleness. She is the goddess of the stages of women: birth, puberty, and menopause. Her maleness gave an independent, aggressive, logical, and goal oriented personality. Thus, she/he is about the perfect balance of female/male energy in the human. This beautiful warrior spirit had raised her silver arrow, aimed it straight, and compassionately hit her mark.

There is much about this quest that could never be told because there are no words for it. There are never words for the revelations of direct experience, only feeble attempts. Why do we forget who we Really are? Why aren't we just born, knowing who we are? Because that would eliminate direct experience. We would miss the creative process. We don't really know something until we have experienced it. The Creator knows all because the creator is directly experiencing through all that it creates. The Creator is in All and the All is in the Creator. We are being given the same gift, to experience the effects of what we create!

The quest in the lodge lasted about two and a half days. When I came out, my teacher was sitting by the fire. He shared with me some of the things that he had observed outside the lodge such as animals and weather patterns. I told him about my attempt to get out of the lodge, but that I could not find the door. He only laughed and said, "There was no way she was going to let you leave!"

It was only during the writing of this book that another connection had been made. I wanted to look up the word artemisia to find its derivation. I found out that the plant had been named after the Greek goddess, Artemis. She was the twin to Apollo and the daughter to Zeus and Leto. She was celebrated in the orient as the Goddess of the Moon, Goddess of the Hunt, Goddess of Women. Artemis was the first born. She helped her mother Leto give birth to her twin brother, thus she is associated with midwifery. Artemis asked her father Zeus if she could remain eternally youthful and virginal. She was at home in the wilderness and the protector of small animals. Poseidon crafted her a silver bow and arrow. Artemis dressed in a tunic with a bow and arrow over her shoulder looking very boyish. Her precocious ways kept her values chaste. They were molded from within by her own curiosity. She encourages us to reflect in our root identity and not that given to us through culture, sex or family.

None of this information had ever been consciously known to me. I was not a history buff nor did I have interest in mythology. There are no coincidences. The spirit of artemisia tridentata (sacred sage) had appeared to me in the form of Artemis, the Greek goddess. I completely trust that this form is what I needed to see in order to receive the messages that sage had for me.

As far as the antics that my teacher had gone through prior to the quest, I was told that I had been the butt of the joke with my Navajo family. They were all to familiar with my fierce, warrior, bulldog attitude of not letting go once I bit into something. As always, this has its benefits and its downfalls. My need to control, manipulate, and direct the play of my life had to die. Their buffoonery was an attempt to push me to the limits of my control issues. In their wisdom they knew what my next step was about... surrender totally to the shamanic death. To meet with the spirit of a warrior plant as strong as artemisia, meant just that. Artemisia is the ultimate purifier in the physical realm as well as the spiritual. Up until then, I only had a superficial relationship with artemisia. I knew many of her healing attributes both physically and ceremonially. But this most deep inner death and rebirth was her true gift to me.

This quest had me realize the strength of the ego and just how powerful it is. The more we allow the ego to direct our life, the more we are missing the deeper meaning of life. We lose the childlike purity that is in awe of life itself. Have we forgotten that LIFE is a miracle? A miracle is defined in Webster's dictionary as an extraordinary event attributed to some supernatural agency. How does it all happen? How does the Great Mystery create? What is the meaning of life?

These are all extraordinary events that must be controlled by a supernatural agency, because no one knows how Life happens!! When we don't find our intuition and trust it, we miss the subtleties, the small miracles, and we miss the fact that guidance is walking along side of us all the time. We don't have ears to hear their voices or the intuitive abilities to read the signs when the ego is in control. When things seem to be going awry in our life it is because the ego is in control. It has ushered in fear and confusion. If you look back at a difficult situation in your life, and you are very honest with yourself, you will say "Yes, there were signals, red flags, omens that I ignored." They are always there for everyone. That is guidance trying to get our attention. If your intuition is fully opened and aware, you immediately see these signs and you (the ego) surrender to that guidance, avoiding the big potholes of life and a lot of suffering.

Without the ability to read the warning signs of life, we are in our own way. We were given the gift of free will so that we have the ability to co-create our lives. To know and experience what "creating" is. This is the grace of Great Mystery. The Great Mystery is constantly creating and allowing us also to experience the ability to create. The choices that we make take us down the road of direct experience. These direct experiences are what paint the backdrop of this lifetime and allow us to work out karmic obligations. Free will is good, but it also has given the ego a place to reside. Our job is to recognize it and tame it so that the ego works for us and we are not working for the ego!! This is the wilderness that must be traversed if the human species wants the answers to the ultimate question, Who am I?

The ego doesn't want you to know who you are because then the Truth would be known and the ego would be tamed.

Tame the ego and free the suffering.

Silver Wolf Walks Alone

Part Three

Searching for the Soul

Care of the soul is a sacred act.

Silver Wolf Walks Alone

The greatest challenge of the 21st century will be to unearth the soul. It has been neglected, abused, denied expression, and its existence questioned. Human life is inherently spiritual and eternal. But through man's own ego, we have created a life, through the gift of free will, that has brought the intellectual and physical life to the forefront. Our true purpose has been buried.

Searching for the Soul has been my preoccupation since childhood. At the age of 10 my parents and I moved to the country. It is then that my closeness with nature began to stir questions deep inside. I would sit on top of my pigeon coop and watch the pigeons fly. "Why can't I fly?" I would wonder. I decided that if I could fly, I might fly away and then who would care for the pigeons? As I got older and went to college I wanted to know why I was here. I wanted to know who God was. Jung said, "I don't believe in God, I know God." Well, if he could, I could!

I could have continued to travel to Taos and live in a more comfortable, convenient, and safe environment back in Virginia. But once again that howl of the wolf was loud and clear... let me out to run free... I knew It was time again for change. Richmond had been good to me and it felt like my lessons there were finished. Life had become very predictable. My days consisted of running my business, a Native American art & craft store. My evenings were filled with classes that I taught, or my own continuous education. My daughter was grown and spending most of her time building her own life. I found that upon review of my life, I had found a certain comfort in Richmond. After 17 years, I finally could go anywhere and I knew people and they knew me.

I was in my mid-forties, single, and just making it financially. My business had peaked and was now leveling off. I could move out West now, or borrow a lot of money and make another commitment to staying with WolfWalker in Richmond. Staying was the ego saying, "Be safe and comfortable, don't rock the boat." Something inside me would never be happy if I did that. If I opted for safety (an illusion) I would miss out on spiritual growth.

It is said that the Creator will not give you anything you can not handle. That does NOT mean he will eliminate challenges from your life. My big decision was the same one that I came across 10 years earlier. Which path do I take? The one most traveled, or the road not taken? For some people, safety and routine is a way of life and they learn from it. For me, it has never been that way. It is the adventure of change and transformation. I have known since childhood that it is my inner wilderness that I must explore and understand and that how I express my outer life (that of making a living, etc.) is secondary. Mastery of self would make me also a master of life.

I have had many teachers that have been mirrors for me. My Navajo guide used the purification lodge and ceremony to reinforce in me, the inner quest. Through him I learned much about the elements and how they healed in the purification lodge. He reinforced in me the need to remember the primal self and celebrate the wild woman. But most of all, he was my guide into the Dark Night of the Soul. A wise teacher will only be a mirror that reflects to the student where they are at, thus enabling the student to be an active part in her own healing.

Throughout time we have been trying to define, locate, understand touch, or see the soul. It can't be located because it has no physical address and its definition seems to be ever changing. For the sake of my readers I will say that the soul is that part of us which is unseparated from the Creator and takes on a physical form in order for the soul to grow to self realization.

Plato said, "If we are to have clear knowledge of anything, we must be liberated from the body and contemplate things with the soul alone."

The Candomble, an African/Brazilian religion, believes that the soul is a combination of the physical and spiritual bodies. God, or Olorum, creates humans by gathering the elements from nature to make the physical body, or the emi. He shapes the body and then blows spiritual life into the top of the head to create the ori, or our spirit. These aspects work together during the physical life until death. Upon death your physical body is returned to Olorum immediately and the spirit returns after seven days. Olorum then takes the ori and blows it into the head of a newborn in your family. This way the ori always stays in the family being passed from one person to the other.

There is a Native American story about the creation of the human soul.

The Creator gathered all of creation and said, "I want to hide something from the humans until they are ready for it."

The eagle said, "Give it to me, I will take it to the moon."

The creator said, "No. One day they will go there and find it."

The salmon said, "I will hide it on the bottom of the ocean."

The Creator said "No. They will go there too."

The buffalo said, "I will bury it on the great plains."

The creator said, "They will cut into the skin of the Mother and find it even there."

Then Grandmother Mole, who lives in the breast of Mother Earth, and who has no physical eyes but sees with spiritual eyes, said, "Put it inside them for they will never look there."

And the Creator said, "It is done."

It is long past due that the search for the soul begins. The secret is out. Look inside for your Truth and happiness. Soul neglect is epidemic throughout the world. When we neglect the soul we create obsessions, addictions, violence, and most of all a loss of meaning for life. When we abuse children through child labor, child pornography, view them as just a commodity, play upon their innocence, and target them as potential customers of questionable products, we are seeing the worst of human society. We are seeing the beginning of a "soulless society."

This is the age of artemisia. She has never been needed more to purify and cleanse the ego, which has buried our true nature. To repair the damage to the soul we must bring back an awe and gratitude for all creation. Nature and all her glory can make our ordinary life extraordinary by giving it depth and value.

Though we are God's sons and daughters, we do not yet realize it........

Meister Eckhart

Intuition and the Inner Voice

My inside, listen to me, the greatest spirit -
the Teacher, is near, wake up!
Run to his feet -
He is standing close to your head right now.
You have slept for millions of years.
Why not wake up this morning?

Kabir

The question asked most is how do you know which voice is that of your intuition. Which one of the many voices in my head is the truth?

How can one listen to the inner voice if it can't be recognized? This is one of the greatest losses to the human society today. By losing touch with our inner voice we have lost a direct line of communication with the Divine. From the divine comes only the truth. Since the beginning, we have been on a journey exploring the illusion that power is outside of us. Something that we must acquire through education, work, or money. That is not the truth of the matter. We were all given the Truth when we were created. It is within us waiting to be recognized by us.

Hildegarde of Bingen was a 12th century German nun and mystic. She began having inspired visions at the age of six. Her many texts reveal the information that exposed her holistic approach to healing. Her medical knowledge and abilities to heal came as a facet of her spiritual work. She received remedies that included herbs, foods, gems, minerals, animal parts, fasting, blood letting, saunas, rest, exercise, from the voice within or divine inspiration. She was not formally educated, yet her knowledge and talents were extensive. Hildegarde was also an artist, psychologist, healer, and composer/musician. She is an excellent example of someone who received clear Truth because she recognized the still small voice within her and did not question it. She lived a simple, clean and full life.

To recognize the inner voice, the higher self, or intuition we must Know Thyself. It is a craft that we must tend to in a conscious and regular manner like a gardener tends her plants. To know thyself is to recognize that we are more than our bodies and that we are far more than just our five senses. Our intuitive abilities ARE the voice of the Divine. It is the voice of the unseen guides and teachers that we all have. We are not alone. To judge this world and its activities by what we see, hear, taste, touch, and smell will never give us answers to all the Great Mysteries or miracles that surround us. Getting in touch with our intuitive abilities seems difficult but there are many paths to this goal. Like anything else, you must set an intention, take responsibility for your actions (and non-actions), and proceed with trust in the process. We learn in school, techniques to discipline the mind such as studying and repetition. To discipline the intuition, there are also techniques.

The first discipline is, know yourself. A curandero once said "To heal the body, prepare the mind. Above all, my life has been an ongoing education in self-knowledge. Once we truly know ourselves, we are all healers."

Lau Tzu said, "The Master travels all day without leaving home."

Clearing your emotional field is key. Being emotionally congested blocks the Truth from coming through. We are continuously getting messages from Divine sources, but we filter them through all the emotional garbage that we carry with us. This "garbage" is from past incarnations that we bring back with us in order to heal that part of the soul. Do not think of karma as a fixed destiny.

Instead, understand that it is an accumulation of tendencies that can lock us into behavior patterns that repeat themselves over and over. The garbage is also that which we (our personality or ego) are creating now that relates back to the patterns we brought in with us. Don't you get tired of your stories? Do you find yourself telling the victim stories over and over again? Whether you are looking for sympathy, or glory, or understanding by telling the woe is me story, it is time to stop it. "This happened to me therefore I am like this... or he did this to me...or I can't because..." This is not in alignment with the Truth. Garbage is everything that creates fear, anger, resentment, separation, and guilt. If it is an action which can harm now or in the future, it is garbage. We all carry a lot of garbage with us. We are all here to heal this load. It happens when one day we wake up and say "Let go of the story."

Only the day dawns to which we are awake....

Thoreau

How did we loose the ability to know the inner voice? By creating a multitude of voices inside our heads. These voices are a culmination of all the experiences in our lives which we react to with fear, judgment, and guilt. These are the experiences which may have caused grief and pain and we have not come to forgive and let go.

We have also blocked the inner voice by creating around us, a field of continuous humming... the noise of all the external stimuli that we have created in the form of electrical gadgets. Walk throughout your home and start to notice the hum of appliances, radios, computers, faxes, telephones, games. We tend to blank it out but the humming is effecting our bodies. We are sensitive beings and respond consciously and unconsciously to the stimuli that is around us. These insidious invaders do not honor the fact that our brains store all this stimuli like a computer. Like any outlet, if we overload, we blow a fuse and the system is no longer operating at its maximum.

The media also invades our minds with a lot of negative propaganda. I once met a psychic that refused to read or listen to any media. She did not educate herself on any topic, yet her readings were very clear. She felt that the road to her higher self would get littered with garbage when she started to fill it with unnecessary information. "Too many voices, she would say... All the information I need is already inside. Just got to listen to it..."

If your mind isn't clouded
with unnecessary things,
this is the best season
of your life.

Wu-Min

We have also lost the ability to know the inner voice because we have lost our connection to the greater web - Nature. Hundreds of years ago, most of the day was spent tending to daily needs, such as gathering food or repairing the family dwelling. The evenings were spent near the fire telling stories, playing instruments, of just being quiet. People sat on the ground, washed in the rivers, worked in the sun or rain, ate fruits and vegetables from their own gardens. They were much closer to reading the signs that nature gave us and using a sixth sense-intuition. How many times have you sat outside and spent time with the stars or walked the woods noticing what grew where and why. Can you navigate your world by knowing the four directions, the stars, or the winds? Learn to navigate your environment through natural means.

Why is it that so many people today are seeking answers from sources outside themselves? Because they don't know which voice to listen to. And why is it that so many people are finding these answers with indigenous peoples or gurus and masters of the Far East? Take a good look at how these people live their lives... simply and close to the earth.

**Direct your right eye inward,
and you'll find a thousand regions
in your mind yet undiscovered.
Travel them and be expert in
home-cosmography.**

Thoreau

Quieting the mind is an exercise that we all need to develop in order to get closer to the inner voice of our intuition. Intuition is a knowing or sensing without the use of a rational process. We have all experienced it one time or another and it was always right. We recognize it as a quiet knowing that appears immediately in the form of a feeling or voice. If we are attuned to that voice and can distinguish it from the other voices, then we have the greatest guide we could ask for in this life.

To recognize the voice of intuition, spend time with all the voices inside of you. Which of these voices are those of your parents, or the voice of fear and judgment? The wounded child or the victim? Which voices are negative and heavy. This is a difficult and time consuming practice, but it helps. As we clean house, we can start to look out through clear windows. Identify the voices. Which ones show up in certain circumstances over and over? Were they correct? Think back to moments in your life when a voice came into your head and said, "don't go there." But you did, and you got burned. You find yourself saying, "I knew I shouldn't have gone there!" The real Truth to any question IS inside of us. It is buried for many of us, but it is there.

**Do you have the patience to wait til
your mud settles and the water is clear?
Can you remain unmoving til
the right action arises by itself?**

Lao Tzu

My teacher tried very hard to show me how my intuitive abilities were cloaked by my life experiences and patterns that had developed. The following story is an example....

I once ate a poisonous mushroom. The person I was with seemed to be competent and trustworthy. The first mushroom he picked and identified I got no "hit" from and we took a small taste. I never hesitated. The second mushroom he picked looked very much like the first but when he opened it, I immediately got a knowing... a hesitation about this one. The voice of the mushroom sent a message to me and it was instantly known in my consciousness that the mushroom could not be eaten. The message was small and quiet. It did not shout at me. It happened as fast or faster than any computer. I never should have ignored it. As fast as that knowing came I should have voiced my feeling and put the mushroom down. Instead, I let my rational brain talk louder than the intuitive brain. I did end up in the emergency room of the hospital sicker than I had ever been. On the way to the hospital I called on Artemisia in her warrior form and asked for help. I acknowledged that I had been negligent in honoring the voice of the mushroom and of my knowing. I was not interested in leaving the planet just yet, and was willing to receive all the help I could get. My reaction to the poison was over in 24 hours. My friends reaction was over in about a week.

This life experience could send two messages. Never eat wild mushrooms again, or listen to the still small voice within. My rational mind said to never eat a wild mushroom again. My teacher would have said, "Don't let this experience cloud your intuitive voice. It was there and you heard it. You chose not to act upon it." I am not advocating the ingestion of wild mushrooms as a way to test the inner voice. It is a very tricky process to identify mushrooms and even experts can make mistakes.

The second discipline is diet. Yes, we are what we eat. You are hearing it from every direction these days. Eat and exercise in a healthy manner. We are only as good as our physical temple. Christ, Buddha, Gandhi, Hildegarde of Bingen, and The Dalai Lama, have all incorporated fasts and cleanses as a regular part of their spiritual practices. The indigenous peoples also used fasts or specific plant diets to gain spiritual knowledge. These fasts and cleanses clear us of our addictions. Addictions are not just physical, they are spiritual. They also serve as emotional crutches which blur any clear vision.

Caffeine, sugar, drugs, alcohol, etc. have become comfortable bed-fellows, because they are easily available and socially acceptable. When you choose to do what it takes to raise your vibrations, so that you are radiating more towards your true soul purpose, rather than the needs of the personality of this lifetime, a dramatic shift in nutrition is often required. If we release negative eating habits and take on the habits of eating certain foods that are much higher in vibration, a physical cleansing takes place. This allows the body to operate at a higher vibration, opening the door to our intuition or higher self. Most of the person's personality may not want to do that, but the ten percent that is fighting to claim wholeness can have more ultimate power than the ninety percent that is fighting to remain unconscious. When you align with that ten percent you open the doorway to your guides and all the unseen help of the Universe. You are helping them help you.

I am not going to dictate a diet to you. Find that which you know to be the best healthy food for you. Some people know they operate best as vegetarians and some people know that they need varying amounts of meat. What we can all agree on is that addictions are known to be harmful to body and soul. Come to terms with yours and make an agreement to let them go. I personally prefer a vegetarian diet, but there are times when meat is needed intuitively, and I respond to that. I do not use tobacco, alcohol, drugs, or stimulants. Some caffeine in the form of green tea or an occasional cup of organic coffee, may be your choice. I participate in regular cleanses and do spiritually oriented fasts.

The third discipline is Trust. If you are a vessel and your intention is to hear that intuitive voice, you will. Be willing to hear and trust what is being said. These messages are quite often denied, because they tell us of changes that have to be made in our lives. Remember that with any change there is growth.

In developing your intuition you will develop a refined sensitivity to the hidden meaning of your focus. Nature will reveal her innermost secrets to those who prepare well. Hildegarde of Bingen said, "In all creation, trees, plants, animals and gem stones, there are hidden secret powers to which no person can know unless they are revealed by God." To Hildegarde they were revealed, because she prepared well. What I learned from Hildegarde was that she recognized the pure voice of intuition and did not hesitate to accept it.

In developing my intuition I would trust what I had heard when asking sage for information. The large bushes around my home have given me information many times. I live on the mesa West of the Rio Grande Gorge. It is high altitude desert, dry, seasonally windy, strewn with volcanic rock that was pushed out of the shield volcanoes a million years ago to the southwest of me. My home is "built upon a rock" which was too big to be removed by the backhoe. When the backhoe driver said that he needed to dynamite the rock bed out I was saddened. I wanted to build my home consciously and with as little disturbance to the land and its inhabitants as possible. I went to the grandmother sage and asked what to do. The message was "Build your home upon the rock." I listened and decided to figure out what that meant later. The backhoe driver said "You will have problems when you try to lay the cement block foundation." No problems arose because I integrated the rock into the cement block foundation. The Northwest corner of the house sits upon the rock and part of it protrudes up from the ground outside of the house to remind me that listening and non-doing saved the land from a great shock. Time and again I ask for guidance from these friends and I trust.

The earth should not be injured.
The earth should not be destroyed.
As often as the elements of the world
are violated by ill-treatment,
so God, will cleanse them.
God will cleanse them through the sufferings,
through the hardships of humankind to use.
But if misused,
God's justice permits Creation to punish humanity.

Hildegarde of Bingen

Artemisia and Her Forms

Anyone who has accustomed himself
to regard the life of any living creature
as worthless
is in danger of arriving also at the idea
of worthless human lives...

Albert Schweitzer

There are many different ways in which you can work with artemisia or any plant. I have tried the following ways, depending on the situation: sitting with the fresh plant still in the ground; direct intuition without any form of the plant in my surroundings; fresh picked and laid in the sweat lodge; dried and burned as a form of purification; as a flower essence; as an essential oil; as a poultice; and as a tea. I never pass up an opportunity to connect with this special plant because I have received realizations about self and mundane information time and again. You will also find other ways yourself. Artemisia is my chief spirit plant. Many times she has told me to use other plants and even other ways in which to heal.

My favorite way to use sage is in lining the floor of the sweat lodge with the fresh cut plant. The heat of the rocks and the water create a steam that releases the volatile compounds of the plant and the lodge and the people are permeated with the aroma and oil of the plant. I also like to use the essential oil of artemisia by applying it directly to me or putting it in a room diffuser. I find essential oils to be a very good way for people who do not have access to fresh plants to establish a relationship with herbs and plants.

Essential oils are the properties of plants, flowers, trees, roots, bushes, or seeds which come from the volatile liquids of each. In the essential oils are the vitamins, minerals, enzymes, and hormones of the plants. They are called essential because it was thought that each oil represented the essence of the plant from which it was obtained. Artemisia is usually steam distilled, which means that hot steam is passed over the plant tissues and the volatile compounds evaporate and are then condensed in water. Not only do essential oils contain oxygenating molecules, but also have a bioelectrical frequency. We and everything else has a frequency that can be measured. Essential oils have a very high frequency, higher than herbs or food. Since this method (connecting with the spirit of divine essence of a plant) is an intuitive process, everyone will have a different experience. The plant may not appear in the same form to everyone. But what may happen is that two or more people will get similar guidance from the same plant. They can also receive different messages from the same plant. Don't get frustrated. Trust that the information is accurate and you will know when you have applied the information by the results. As in every activity, you will get better and more discriminating in your interpretations. Be diligent in practicing the three aspects of hearing the intuitive voice. Healthy people usually have a frequency of 62 - 78 Hz.. Disease begins at 58 Hz.. Because essential oils have a frequency higher than most diseases, they create an environment in which disease, bacteria, virus, and fungus can not live.

Priests, medicine people, and physicians have used essential oils for thousands of years. The Bible has made references to oils. Frankincense, myrrh, rosemary, hyssop and spikenard were used for the anointing and healing of the sick. Oils were used to protect from disease or to cure. The oils brought to the Christ child had immuno-stimulating properties. The oldest use of oils was for emotional and spiritual purposes. The inhalation of oils worked directly on the sense of smell which affects the limbic system of the brain. The oil triggers millions of electrical signals that form coded messages which are then dispatched to various areas of the body. The production of endorphins are increased and the entire body can move to a better state of health. Try placing artemisia or other oils on your feet and see if you don't sense a change in the body or mind. Try putting different essential oils in a room diffuser. They can purify the air by removing toxins. They also increase the oxygen of the air and negative ions.

Using artemisia as a flower essence can also be a wonderful tool in practicing a total intuitive experience. I recommend sage for anyone dealing with depression. Depression is no longer having faith or hope. These are inherently ours, and can never be taken away. It is the ego who creeps in during weak moments and hides these aspects of the human from herself. The soul is always connected to us and the divine. Unearth her with sage! Flower essence therapy is mostly used as a therapy for the soul. Remember that we are far more than just a human body. That is actually a very small aspect of who we really are. Use sage for addictions. They are rooted in a spiritual imbalance, but often manifest in the physical body. Disease is always an imbalance in one or more of the bodies - emotional , physical, or mental. Flower essence can be placed on the chakra centers or spritzed around the etheric body.

I have known people who have made tremendous shifts in consciousness by intuitively requesting a favorite flower to help them, not knowing what that flower's essential healing gift was.

An artist friend of mine was blocked creatively. She had not been able to paint for months due to an exhaustive work schedule. When she did make time, she got depressed because nothing flowed, and time was limited. I suggested that she try doing something else that was creative but could be accomplished in a short period of time. She had always wanted to try her hand at a small flower garden and she loved working with colors. We sat for a moment and I asked her to pick a favorite flower. It was iris. She got very excited about the thought of planting a garden that was all purple and blue and she could do it over a weekend. A few days later I visited her and brought a few flower essences. She picked a bottle without knowing its label. Of course, it was iris. She thought it was a funny coincidence until the next "coincidence" was unfolded. Iris works with a pattern imbalance in creativity - the lack of creativity in life and feeling too weighed down by everyday duties!! She used the flower essence for a few weeks. I got a call from her with a report that she had quit her job. She recognized that feeding her spirit was more important than the extra bucks. She was back to painting and a part-time job at a local nursery.

Help is there for us. It comes to us in a multitude of ways. This woman now has a beautiful collection of works she has painted of iris in a Japanese motif. What an honoring of this spirit and trust in oneself!

Part Four

Meeting Doubt on the Path

Small doubt,
small enlightenment:
big doubt,
big enlightenment.

Nine Mountains

Everyone experiences doubt and fear along the road of life. Even those of us who try to put our spiritual practices in balance with our every day work schedule get frustrated and wonder if we are really making progress. One does not have a better road to enlightenment than the other. You and I have as much of a chance of self-realization as the monk in the cave. There are many people in monasteries who never reach a state of self-realization just as in lay society. Artemis told me that healing is the inner path. Enlightenment is being aware in every moment, not lamenting over the past or anticipating the future. Find peace in every moment. When one can fall into any moment with no feeling of suffering you are on the right path. When plans change and you ride with it instead of being attached to "the plan" you are on your way.

One of our greatest teachers, the Buddha, was born into the lap of royalty. Nothing was denied him in the material world. He experienced the extreme end of material riches. Yet he longed to see what lay outside the walls of the palace. When he saw that the world outside of the palace lacked material goods, and people suffered from poverty, disease, and death, he left the palace and became an ascetic monk determined to reach enlightenment as quickly as possible for the benefit of the world. After experiencing extreme austerity for six years the Buddha realized that enlightenment was not to be found in either extreme. The seeker must move away from both extremes to a middle way. Attachment is still attachment whether it be to self-indulgence or self-inflicted abuse.

The greatest teachers are those who have met and fallen into these challenges only to die and resurrect time and time again. What have they done that perhaps we have not? Detachment to controlling the outcome! Each new set of circumstances calls for a new surrender. One must not even become attached to how we surrender. One pearl of truth is that everything in this universe is ever-changing. Thus, it is a constant cycle of death and rebirth. Just as Christ knew of his eminent death, he did not fight it or become victim of it. His total surrender to it came in his wisdom of knowing a great rebirth would also follow.

This journey is bottomless. This is where the mystery and awe of life exists. Each moment is bottomless. Allow yourself to fall into each moment, and then the next, and the next, and the next. Rest at ease in each moment. We are both the subject and the object of the moment. It is only the illusion of duality that keeps us separate in the moment.

In that moment at the lodge, where I was going to be slain by the arrow, I fell into that bottomless stillness that came over me. In the falling came the knowing that I was All of It. I was the personality Silver Wolf; and I was Artemis; and I was the welcomed piercing arrow that crucified the illusions in my life. In that death came the resurrection and my freedom. I am..... there are no more powerful words than "I am."

Some questions have been asked of me a lot since I told the story of this quest, including: "How do you know if you are still trying to control the situation?" and "How do you know if you have truly died to the situation or concept at hand?" I will tell you from my experience. You have not "died" if there is not a resurrection. If you have come from a situation still attached to anger, revenge, fear of what comes next, or the need to control the outcome, you are not dead yet, you are still dying, and resisting the death. Here is where the emotional and mental suffering happens. Now you are hanging on to death for fear of what might lie behind death itself!! What lies behind death is resurrection! There is NO suffering in the resurrection, only stillness in the penetrating light of awareness... Awareness of the Truth.

When doubt arises know that it too, will fall away, sit with it. Be Still. There is nothing to be done. Just as seasons come and go, the sun rises and sets, we are born, grow old and die, only to be born again, everything, has its rhythm.

There are certain principles of the universe, when understood, make clearer the understanding of why things happen. The principle of rhythm is a good one to look at when doubt arises. All spiritual journeys entail mountains and valleys, moments of struggle and moments of relaxation. The truth of the matter is that this up and down journey of life doesn't mysteriously end. Rhythm is an action and reaction, a back and forth, a rising and sinking that is manifested in all phenomena of the Universe. Even in our thoughts. That old adage of "sleep on it" is good advice. How many times did you go to bed confused only to wake up the next morning with an answer? The beauty of this non-ending is we are consistently given the opportunity to experience all that is without attachment to the suffering. I am not saying that you will not experience suffering. I am saying that you do not have to remain attached to the suffering. Let it go. Only fear keeps you hanging on to the suffering. Living in the desert has shown me more about rhythm than any other experience. You can not escape the elements here. The patterns of the seasons, the wind, the rains, the migrations of the animals, can make your life miserable or teach you one of the great universal truths... rhythm. If you watch closely it can even be seen in peoples thoughts.

When people come to visit me here at my home. I am very aware of a rhythm between the mind and the no mind. I have an incredible 360° view. The greatest unobstructed view is a distance that extends for 150 miles North of me. First, people lose any sense of "self" or "ego" and they melt into this immensity of nature. They become one with it. There is a momentary stillness and peace. This stillness is the Truth of who we are, not the continual chatter of the mind/ego. The ego has momentarily taken a backseat. As we all know, it is almost impossible to keep the mind still for more than a minute because its nature is thought. Eventually the pendulum swings back and the visitor becomes aware of the self again. When the conversation begins, the ego wants control back, and is upset that it was ignored for a moment, and it does that by introducing the old friend - fear. This happens in such an insidious manner that we are not conscious of the process. The conversation moves to, "Are there snakes or spiders or scorpions here? Don't you get scared being all alone out here? Don't you miss the trees or grass or rain? Its so quiet. Do you miss the activity of the city? There is nothing out here but sage, rock and dirt!" The original stillness and awe is clouded by fear. The ego/self is again struggling for control because, for a few minutes they forgot self and embraced the awe of oneness. Fear did not exist. Danger was neither felt nor seen. What changed in that moment to the next? It wasn't anything in the outside landscape. The change occurred in the inner landscape. They become aware again of "I". The only way "I" knows how too stay in control is to start grasping for concepts of duality.

It is no wonder why Christ or other questors go to the desert to meet the Dark Night of the Soul. Your fears are welcomed and there is no place to hide and no place to run. Wherever you go there you are. The desert intensifies this experience as does the existence of artemisia. She welcomes your fears and illusions. All plants have their gifts. It just takes time, intention, and a clear channel to access this information.

My quest with this great being, artemisia (sage) will be lifelong. She is as much me as I am her. Her gift to the world is to crucify the egotistical illusions we have about self and the world, and to grant us clear vision so that the spirit we think we are IS.

da' Naho

EPILOGUE

WOLF MEDICINE

the still small voice within...
whispering... elusive... disappearing...
what did you say?

that howling... getting louder...
ahh... I heard you this day!

this voice...
this feeling... that wells up from deep deep inside...
so familiar, ancient, and wise

if you come again... I shall look into your eyes...
and know... that our spirit flies!

Silver Wolf Walks Alone

Artemisia tridentata (sage), full of wisdom, is for me the great purifier of illusion. She is also the balancer of male and femaleness. We have all known that for hundreds of years the scales have been tilted to serve male domination. The world, in its own great rhythm, has been trying to balance those scales and sends us great gifts in consciousness. We have experienced the Womens Liberation Movement take a huge leap in the 1970's. This shifting and sharing of power has come because of the imbalance of energies here on earth. When a system is out of balance, that same system will reach a point where it will then seek to balance itself. This is called entropy.

Many prophecies have indicated that a balancing and reshaping of the earth and our lives is at hand. The Virginia psychic and prophet Edgar Cayce said that "entropy of the masculine and feminine energy would begin in 1933... soul of an androgynous nature would enter the new born bodies here on earth." This would continue for about 100 years helping to bring balance back to the earth.

My experience with the androgynous Artemis only reinforces this observation. All of us are on the threshold of immense change. One that I am grateful to be a part of. The balancing is not just pertinent to male/female, but to all aspects of the spirit. I give thanks to the Great Spirit of this medicinal plant and all her uses. I am especially grateful for the all encompassing healing abilities of this plant in the purification lodge. This is her realm and this is where you will feel the true essence of this plant. If you are ready to recognize the Truth of your essence she will guide you there!

Other books available:

Sacred Sage How it Heals

Smudge Pack ©

To order copies of this book:

call 575-737-5686

or

order from the website

www.wolfwalkercollection.com